Walks
Yorkshire Dales
RIBBLESDALE

Mary Welsh

A QUESTA Guide

© Mary Welsh 2007

ISBN 978-1-898808-17-6

PUBLISHER'S NOTE
It is the responsibility of parents when out walking with children to supervise them and to make judgements about whether any part of a walk is unsuitable for them.

Readers are advised that while the author has made every effort to ensure the accuracy of this guidebook, changes can occur which may affect the contents. The Publishers would welcome notes of any changes you find.

Neither the author nor Questa Publishing Limited can accept responsibility for any inaccuracies, or for any injuries or damage that may occur while following the routes in this book.

Maps:
The maps accompanying the walks in this book are purely diagrammatic. They are based on maps produced by, and with the permission of,
Harvey Maps.
© Harvey Maps 2005

Published by
Questa Publishing Ltd.
PO Box 520, Bamber Bridge, Lancashire PR5 8LF
and printed by
Carnmor Print, 95/97 London Road, Preston,
Lancashire PR1 4BA

Contents

Introduction	4
Walk 1 Gearstones, Ling Gill and God's Bridge	6
Walk 2 Ribblehead Viaduct and Chapel-le-Dale	10
Walk 3 Colt Park Wood	14
Walk 4 Alum Pot and Long Churn, Selside	18
Walk 5 Horton in Ribblesdale, Sulber Nick, Crummack Dale	21
Walk 6 Horton in Ribblesdale, Hull Pot and Hunt Pot	25
Walk 7 Horton in Ribblesdale and foot of Penyghent	28
Walk 8 Stainforth and Catrigg Force	32
Walk 9 Stainforth Force, Langcliffe and Winskill	35
Walk 10 Attermire Scar and Victoria Cave	38

Introduction

Ribblesdale

The River Ribble, from which the dale takes its name, rises high in the Yorkshire Pennines and passes through some very dramatic countryside. Very soon the river receives water from tributary streams that have passed through potholes, underground passages, deep caves, gorges and over waterfalls. It flows past slate quarries and under delightful footbridges and ancient stone bridges. Eventually it passes through Lancashire and empties its water on the Lancashire coast below Blackpool.

Some of the walks in this book take you over old tracks which, until about 200 years ago, were the only means of traversing this part of Yorkshire. There were no tarmacked roads. The Romans made some of the tracks, and monks made others, tending their great flocks. The tracks were walked by travellers and pedlars. Drovers urged their cattle over them on their way to sales at Gearstones, where there were many walled pastures to prevent the cattle from straying. The tracks were used by 'trains' of packhorses, loaded with goods and each led by a horse with bells on its harness; a young boy would bring up the rear. As you walk the quiet ways of Ribblesdale, it is easy to imagine that you can hear a bell or maybe come upon a train of ponies round the next bend!

Ribblesdale is mainly open countryside. The tree cover is to be found in steep-sided gills, such as Ling Gill, or clinging to Daleside scars, such as Colt Park Wood, out of the reach of hungry sheep. Much of the woodland that once clothed the lower slopes of the hills of the dale was removed during four centuries of sheep grazing, conducted by the monks of the great abbeys of Sawley, Bolton, Fountains and Furness, who owned the land. After the monasteries were dissolved, farmers built enclosing drystone walls. Today farmers still shape the appearance of the dale and hills.

One of the remarkable features of Ribblesdale is the Settle-Carlisle railway, opened in May 1876. It cost £4 million to lay the track through the dale and on to the vale of Eden. In the winter of 1868 a young man named Sharland took ten days to walk from Carlisle to Settle, planning the route the line would take. In November 1869 the first sod was cut and a shanty town for the 2,000 workforce was built on Batty Green at Ribblehead. In Walk 2 you might like to visit the church of St Leonard, Chapel-le-Dale, to see the memorial plaque to those workmen who died in accidents and visit their graves across the road in the little churchyard extension. The spectacular 24-arched Batty Moss viaduct at Ribblehead is seen dramatically from the route of the first walk in this book and passed under in the second.

The tracks and footpaths used in this book make for ideal walking. Start with the easier walks and gradually work up to the more demanding ones when youngsters, for whom this book is compiled, are ready to tackle them. All the walks have interesting places to visit and young people will spot even more than are mentioned here. The views are magnificent. The wildlife reflects the soil and rock below. A gentle introduction to hill walking in such a glorious area will set children off on what could become a compulsive, lifelong and extremely healthy pastime.

During the walk it might be a good time to discuss with the youngsters the following points from

The Country Code
Enjoy the countryside and respect its life and work
Guard against all risk of fire
Fasten all gates
Keep to public paths across farmland
Use gates and stiles to cross fences,
hedges and walls
Leave livestock, crops and machinery alone
Take your litter home. Help to keep all water clean
Protect wildlife, plants and trees
Take special care on country roads
Make no unnecessary noise.

1
Gearstones, Ling Gill and God's Bridge

This is a glorious walk with magnificent views across rolling moorland to the three peaks, Ingleborough, Penyghent and Whernside. The spectacular Ribblehead Viaduct, which carries the Settle Carlisle railway, enhances the walk for much of the way. Some of the tracks, the Dales Way (DW) and the Pennine Way (PW), which sweep over the moorland, are heavily used and have been reinforced by layers of stones. The often grassy Ribble Way (RW) is sometimes wet and difficult to follow, but it has excellent step-stiles, which help you on your return route over the quiet slopes. Youngsters will enjoy map reading and seeking out these stiles.

Start: A large lay-by, west and on the same side as Gearstones Lodge, on the B6255. (GR778799)

Total distance: 10.5km (6½ miles)

Height gain: 210m (660ft)

Difficulty: Moderate. Mainly good tracks except crossing the moorland where paths can be indistinct

1. Walk north-west to pass Gearstones Lodge, a backpackers self catering hostel. Carry on, with care, for nearly half a mile to take the right turn, signposted 'Dales Way footpath to Cam End'. Go through a gate and descend through the next one. Negotiate a tiny ford and then cross the footbridge over Gayle Beck, which soon becomes the River Ribble. Climb on up the rough way, once a Roman road, to step across a small stream, pausing to enjoy the extensive views. Carry on until you reach a three-armed signpost.

2. Turn right to walk the PW, an equally rough track, with the view of the Three Peaks and the viaduct to encourage you on. Remain on the track as it begins to descend a little to arrive at Ling Gill Bridge where the Cam Beck comes tumbling out of the moorland to pass through this delightful hollow. Continue to the information board for Ling Gill nature reserve. Dawdle beside the fenced edge of this magnificent extremely deep limestone gorge. Very soon you are unable to see the beck dancing through the bottom. The grassy slopes close to the

WALKS WITH CHILDREN: RIBBLESDALE

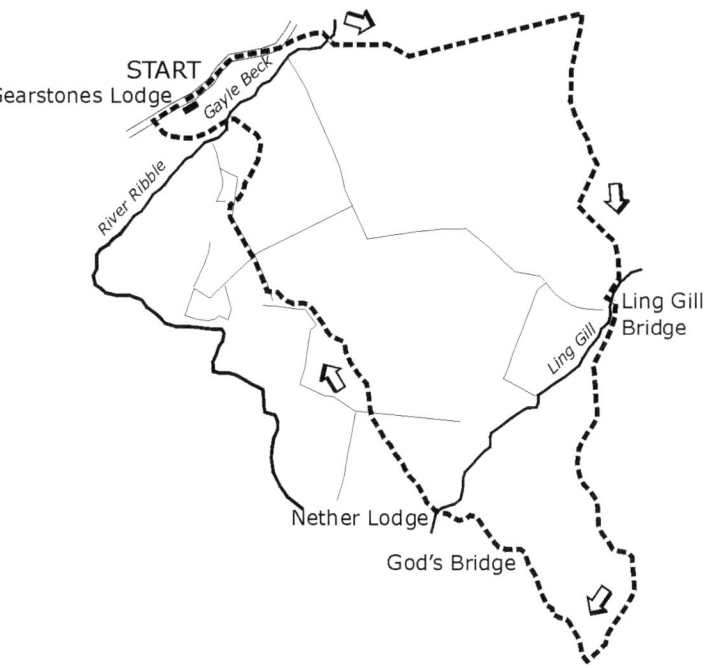

fence are colourful with flowers in summer, a great contrast to the moorland vegetation seen on the first part of the walk. Here you will want to pause.

3. Just before the PW moves away from the gill, a stile gives access to a flattish area above the gill and inside the fence. *Here you are asked to take great care. Young children should be under close control.* Carry on along the track as it gently descends to where there is a signpost and the PW turns sharp left.

4. Leave the PW and take the unmarked gate on the right and begin to descend a reinforced track. Pass the access track to Old Ing, on the left, and carry on down through gentler pasture towards a plantation. Just before it take, on the right, a signposted track, the Ribble Way, for Nether Lodge. Carry on to climb a ladder-stile beside a gate. Stroll on the good track

WALKS WITH CHILDREN: RIBBLESDALE

as it climbs a little and then winds right still climbing, with an enormous expanse of rolling moorland ahead of you. Then where the track ceases, carry on over grass, beside the wall on your left, to reach a walled area and then a stile and a gate. Beyond, wind round right to see God's Bridge, which you have just crossed without noticing. This is a delightful corner and just the place for another break.

5. Then remain in the same pasture and wind half left to view the cleft through which Brow Gill Beck emerges into another delightful leafy hollow. Return the few steps to pick up the continuing grassy way, which soon becomes reinforced and leads to Nether Lodge. As you near the farm, the route on the map has been altered. The path, instead of passing through the farmyard, continues ahead, crosses a new footbridge over Ling Gill Beck, which keeps walkers north, and well away from, the farm and its outbuildings. Follow the signpost that directs you ahead along the Ribble Way and then continue, striking very slightly left across a huge flat pasture, which is damp in places. Then ascend gently to climb a sturdy stile, with duckboarding on either side, over the fence.

6. Descend a little, in the same general direction, to cross a wet hollow, where there are several small streams to step over – or jump. The path is barely visible but in general follow the occasional wheel mark of a quad bike. Then ascend a little and head on to a kink in the wall in the far corner. Here, to the right of a gate is a good stone step-stile over a wall below the low slopes of Tile Hill. Beyond, go on ahead, keeping beside the wall on your left. Very soon a good path emerges and winds on as the wall turns away left. Follow the path as it winds about a little before it arrives at a stone step-stile to the left of a derelict barn, seen clearly ahead.

7. Once over, walk ahead and just beyond the barn, turn right and climb the fine grassy pasture, remaining parallel with the wall on your right, to a wall gap at the top of the slope. Stride on, descending steadily still keeping by the wall, to take a ladder-stile to the right of a barn, belonging to derelict Thorns, a picturesque ruin among its sheltering sycamores. Cross a small pasture, go through a gate and turn right as directed by a lichen–encrusted signpost. Walk a short walled track and then go through a gate or climb the ladder-stile beside it, to wind left, following a clear grassy path. This crosses the slopes and then descends to the side of the young River Ribble.

8. Walk left, downstream, to cross a footbridge. Beyond, walk ahead for a few steps to join a delightful grassy track and stroll left to a stile in the wall corner. Carry on along the excellent trod to come to a ladder-stile that decants you into the lay-by where you have parked.

Along the way

Ling Gill Nature Reserve. Birch, rowan, bird cherry and ash clothe the sides of Ling Gill. This type of woodland is now scarce; the trees have survived because the steep sides of the limestone gorge have prevented access to grazing animals. Beneath the trees there is a rich ground flora, including melancholy thistle, baneberry, globe flower, primroses, bugle, bird's eye and purple orchid. Cam Beck flows through the ravine in a series of waterfalls descending for about 30m as it passes through the gill.

Brow Gill Beck having descended through a narrow tree-lined gill and dropped down a waterfall, flows for a few metres over its rocky bed with pasture on either side. It then disappears under a huge natural 'blockstone', **God's Bridge**, shadowed by an ash. It emerges through a cleft set about with trees and bushes and then hurries on to add its waters to Cam Beck in its race to lose its energy in the River Ribble.

The lovely dale through which these walks pass takes its name from the **River Ribble**. Finding the exact start of the river is puzzling. The Gayle and Cam Becks flow out of the moors and about Gearstones and unite. They are augmented by numerous streams that emerge from underground caverns and the Ribble is born. It begins as Yorkshire river and passes through Lancashire to join the sea below Blackpool.

Several public footpaths converged on **Nether Lodge** – three from the north and two from the south. One that passed through the farmyard was part of the popular Three Peaks route. The footpath also carried the well-used Ribble Way trail. Regular sponsored walks used the route as well. On some weekends, in the summer, 2,000 walkers came through the yard and the farmer was unable to work with his sheep. After widespread consultation, the Yorkshire Dales National Park Authority made a diversion order. As a result the YDNPA has constructed a footbridge over Ling Gill Beck, which the newly diverted footpath crosses. The farmer is delighted at the result as the diversion gives him freedom to work with his sheep in the farmyard on Saturdays and Sundays.

WALKS WITH CHILDREN: RIBBLESDALE

2
Ribblehead Viaduct and Chapel-le-Dale

This gentle walk, through a smiling landscape amid frowning fells, starts close to the Ribblehead Viaduct, which spans the hollow of Batty Moss. It passes two pot holes and then returns over higher ground to walk beside the viaduct once more – all the family can't have too much of a good thing!

Start: From the parking area at the junction of the B6255 and the B6479 (GR764791)

Total distance: 10.5km (6½ miles)

Height gain: 220m (700ft)

Difficulty: Little. An undemanding stroll in pleasant country in the shadow of two Yorkshire giants.

1. Cross the road from the parking area and join a stony track. Follow it as it leads across the moorland to pass between two of the 24 flaring, numbered pillars, of Ribblehead viaduct. Beyond, stroll on the good track through the bleached moorland grass, with sink holes on either side. Pause as you go to look back, south–east, to see Penyghent, to the right, beyond the viaduct. Pass through two gates, close together, and cross a footbridge over Winterscales Beck.

2. Turn left to walk a gated unfenced road. Follow it as it bears left and go on to cross a narrow bridge over the beck again. After 500m look right to see an easy-to-miss small gate in a wall corner. Here leave the road and approach the gate across a short stretch of pasture, with a wall to the right. Beyond the gate, which you are reminded to close, is an indistinct footpath. Follow this to come to the side of the beck. Head for the gate to the right of some horizontal metal poles used to fence off a pothole. Beyond move carefully to the left to see the hollow, under ash and sycamore.

3. Stride over a pleasing pasture, with larch to the right and conifers away to the left, to a gate, which gives access to a very rough walled and hedged track. This leads to Philpin Lane. (If the track is under water, head up left to walk beside the

WALKS WITH CHILDREN: RIBBLESDALE

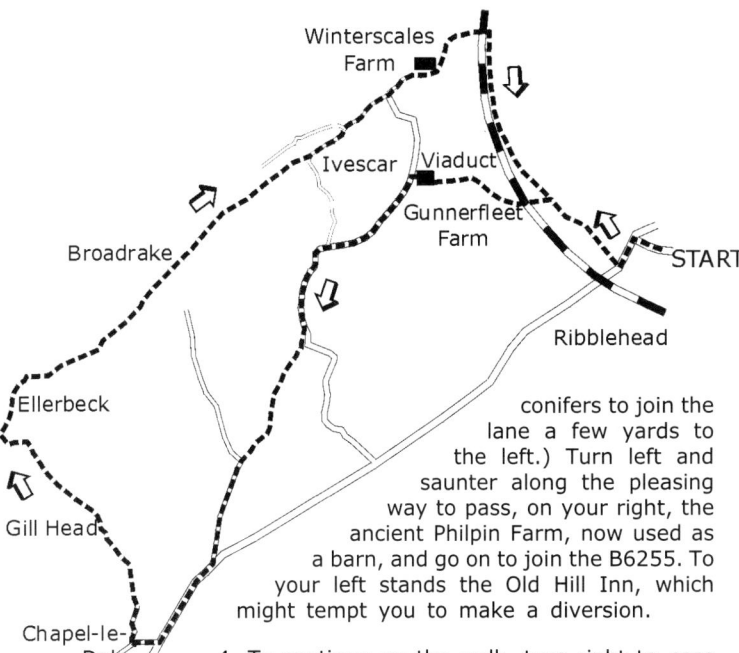

conifers to join the lane a few yards to the left.) Turn left and saunter along the pleasing way to pass, on your right, the ancient Philpin Farm, now used as a barn, and go on to join the B6255. To your left stands the Old Hill Inn, which might tempt you to make a diversion.

4. To continue on the walk, turn right to pass Chapel-le-Dale's old schoolhouse, now used as a bunkhouse and, with care, stride downhill until you can turn right in the direction of the church as directed by a signpost. Dawdle the shadowy lane to visit St Leonard's church. Then leave by the metal kissing gate at the back of the churchyard to join a walled lane that climbs steadily. Just beyond a cattle grid, look right to see the great chasm of Hurtle Pot and go on upwards. *Young children should be under control here*.

5. Where the way divides take the right fork, signposted Ellerbeck. As you go look for a statue on the left. A small plaque says that 'For years a statue stood on this spot. It was vandalised on Saturday August 27, 1983 and was subsequently found in 30ft of water at the bottom of Hurtle Pot. An enthusiastic team of divers made the recovery and it has been erected again as found. It was the creation of the late Charles I'Anson, the well known sculptor and artist. Time will tell if the

WALKS WITH CHILDREN: RIBBLESDALE

spirit of the boggard of Hurtle Pot is now enshrined in the statue.'

6. Continue up the lovely lane, which is edged with moss-covered walls, as it passes through deciduous copses. Go by Gill Head Farm and follow the way as it leads onto the open moor. To your right is a first view of the viaduct, looking, at this distance, too fragile to support even a toy train.

7. At the T-junction turn right in the direction of Deepdale. Go through Ellerbeck farmyard and continue on the reinforced way. To the left lie low scars of limestone and, above, the austere slopes of Whernside. The reinforced way continues past Bruntscar Farm. Beyond, ignore all left and right turns and continue ahead along the bridleway, signposted Winterscales, over pasture to pass Broadrake Farm. Press on ahead along the distinct gated way, enjoying the wide extensive views over the lovely dale. Continue on where the way becomes metalled to pass Ivescar and then its large barns.

8. Stride on and where the lane swings right, go ahead on a reinforced way. Pass Winterscales Farm on your left. Keep beside the wall on your left as you pass two cottages on your right. Go through a gate and carry on the continuing rough muddy track out onto the moor, with the beck to your left. The track comes close to the hurrying water and then swings right to pass under a bridge that carries the Carlisle to Settle railway.

9. Beyond, turn right and follow the good track over the boggy moor, walking parallel with the line. Descend the reinforced slope to join the track, taken at the outset of the walk, to return to your car.

Along the way

Between the viaduct that spans the hollow of Batty Moss and the village of Chapel-le-Dale lies a delightful tract of cultivated land. The south is edged by the B6255 and to its north sprawl the bleak slopes of Whernside. Farms with Norse names like **Winterscales** and **Gunner Fleet** nestle beneath the grim fell, facing the sun. Here limestone outcrops, and ash trees have taken hold. Walled pastures abound, cattle graze peacefully and small streams come and go, disappearing below their limestone beds. One or two narrow unfenced roads pass through this secluded area, which is overlooked to the south by a frowning face of Ingleborough.

WALKS WITH CHILDREN: RIBBLESDALE

The Viaduct. Notice the sturdy cairn erected in 1992, with its large brass plate depicting a Victorian navvy with his pick-axe and a modern day workman with a pneumatic drill. The accompanying legend says that the viaduct was built between 1870 and 1875 and was fully restored, in three stages, between 1988 and 1991. The cairn commemorates both those who toiled to build and those who renovated the viaduct. It also adds a note about the natural tendency of the limestone to flake and fall. Be warned.

Chapel-le-Dale church. Go through the lychgate and then inside to see the plain simple church, with charming stained-glass windows and pleasing carved altar rail. On the back wall is a marble tablet dedicated 'to the memory of those who through accidents lost their lives in constructing the railway works between Settle and Dent Head. This tablet was erected at the joint expense of their fellow workmen and the Midland Railway Company, 1869–1876.'

Two thousand men lived in a **shanty town on Batty Green**. In addition to those who died in accidents constructing the viaduct and Blea Moor tunnel, so many died in a smallpox outbreak that the churchyard had to be enlarged in the 1870s.

For ten days in 1808, at the worst time of the year, the route of the Carlisle to Settle railway was walked by a man named Sharland who originated from Tasmania. As he walked, accompanied by several companions, he planned the route of the line. They weather was atrocious and they had to manage difficult river crossings, even worse bog crossings, awkward gradients, and blizzards. One blizzard marooned them for three weeks on Blea Moor. Eventually the first sod was cut in November of the next year, the navvies working under even more atrocious conditions.

As you walk you might spot a **stoat** relentlessly following the trail of its prey. Look for a long, lithe animal that moves in a succession of low bounds. Its upper parts are reddish-brown, and the underparts tinged with yellow. The tail is the same colour but it invariably has a tuft of long black hairs at its tip. In a snowy winter its coat changes to white. On this walk you might see one running along a stone wall and then disappearing into gaps between the stones, especially if the wall is near a picnic site and there might be scraps to be had. Generally its diet consists of rabbits, mice, voles, small birds, eggs and fish. Its biggest predator is man and despite the speed at which it can race across a road, many die under the wheels of a car.

WALKS WITH CHILDREN: RIBBLESDALE

3
Colt Park Wood

A mile-long stretch of ash woodland, away to your left, comes as a delightful surprise on this walk. The bleak lonely slopes of the Ingleborough massif towers above, but all is gentle and peaceful as you stroll these softer pastures, and pass through short stretches of the woodland, which resounds with birdsong in the spring and is colourful with wild flowers in summer. The magnificent hay meadows about the River Ribble are another delight.

Alas there is a drawback on this walk – some unavoidable road walking. People-carriers delivering potholers to Alum Pot, and wagons in a hurry to deliver their loads from the quarries, use the road. Therefore youngsters should be reminded that though it is generally quiet the wagons are busy all year round and potholers explore all year and therefore care must taken as they walk the short stretches of the B-road.

Start: Large lay-by on the east side of the B6479, 300m before (north of) Gauber farm (GR 772787)

Total distance: 11km (6¾ miles)

Height gain: 150m (395ft)

Difficulty: Generally easy walking, with several little ascents.

1. Walk west along the B-road, using the grassy verge for most of the way. At the top of the hill take the wide track going off right, signposted 'Sleights'. Go past several cottages, once railway dwellings, and carry on over the Settle-Carlisle railway where it passes through a cutting. Pass a fine limekiln and carry on where limestone breaks through the grass and ahead you can see the steep slopes of Park Fell. Head on to pass low limestone scars many with crag-fast ash as you enter the woodland.

2. At the wall of Colt Park house, ignore the ladder-stile ahead and turn left to go through a large gate. Walk on, in summer through the glorious hay meadows, with the woodland away to your left. Go on over three meadows and climb the ladder-stile to the left of Rigg Barn. Bear half left to join a wide grassy trod continuing across the middle of another colourful pasture. At the English Nature board, follow the arrow directing you left.

WALKS WITH CHILDREN: RIBBLESDALE

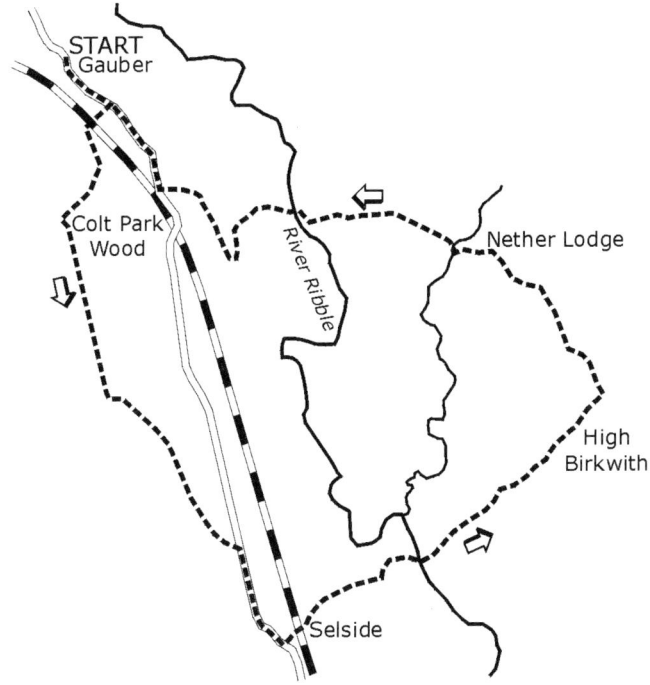

Climb the stile and descend a short rough path over more limestone. At the foot of the path, turn left and then in a few steps wind round, right, to strike diagonally to a ladder-stile over the far wall. Beyond, keep on the same general diagonal over the next two ladder-stiles. Carry on steadily descending, below a low hill to your right, to reach another nature reserve notice board and a gate to the B-road once more.

3. Turn right and walk on to face oncoming traffic, to pass the parking track for Alum Pot. Cross the road here and descend on the grass verge a short distance to reach the hamlet of Selside. You will know that you have arrived by the name plate, which once adorned the local signal box. Just past the post box, turn left, with a telephone box now to your right, to walk a wide track. Stroll on between houses as the way winds right and passes under a railway bridge. Then continue along

WALKS WITH CHILDREN: RIBBLESDALE

a charming walled lane. At the signpost, bear left to come to a gate and another signpost. Beyond the gate, bear right to carry on below a wooded hillock to the right. At this point the footbridge over the River Ribble comes into view.

4. Cross the bridge and walk ahead through a charming hay meadow, with Coppy gill beck to your left. A small plank bridge takes you over a narrow a stream. Walk on through this idyllic flat land. Pass through a gap stile in the wall and then a gate into the farmyard of Low Birkwith. Walk ahead, with the beck to your left and the farmhouse to your right. Wind round with the beck and then look for the stile in the wall, up a steepish slope, on your right. Once through the awkward stile, bear left heading for another stile giving into a long thin belt of trees. Walk ahead for a few steps to take a ladder-stile out of the trees and into a pasture. Swing right to a step stile in the wall, immediately to the left of the last barn of High Birkwith farm to join a road.

5. Turn left and walk the track to go through a gate. Go on climbing to a take a track going off left, signed Nether Lodge. Follow the track to climb a step stile over a wall. Stride on soon to move over to walk beside the wall on your left. Cross a small walled area and go through the gate or climb the ladder-stile. Before you carry on bear round right to see God's Bridge, a huge natural boulder under which flows Brow Gill Beck. Stroll on along the easy-to-walk track and follow it to a gate, on your left, into a small pasture, behind Nether Lodge. Cross the pasture and then the tractor Bridge, signed 'Three Peaks', over Cam Beck. Beyond, wind right through the farm buildings and the side of the farmhouse to climb a ladder-stile to come to two signposts.

6. Turn left and walk the wide white track through the rough pasture of Ingman Lodge. Cross the bridge over the Ribble and follow the track as it winds left, climbs a little, before winding right to go past Lodge Hall, formerly Ingman Lodge, with a datestone 'C W 1687' . Stroll on along the minor road, now tarmacked, to join the B6479. Turn right and using the verges, where possible, return along the road for just over half a mile to the parking lay-by.

Along the Way

The pleasing track runs through a small stretch of **Colt Park Wood** nature reserve before turning left and continuing through colourful hay meadows that lie above the predominant ash woodland thriving on limestone pavement. This fine mile long strip of trees lies on a terrace, 340m up, on the flanks of Park Fell, the northern end of Ingleborough's great mass.

In June **the hay meadows** above Colt Park Wood are unbelievably beautiful. Buttercups predominate and a golden glow enhances a dull day. Among these flowers thrive red clover, eyebright, hay rattle and mouse ear chickweed. The hay meadows beyond the river, below Low Birkwith, are dominated by bistort, a fine upstanding pink flower. These lovely Ribblesdale meadows are left to grow hay and have received virtually no artificial fertiliser and because of this produce an abundance of wild flowers.

Several **limekilns** are passed on this walk, some collapsed, others still almost intact. Inside the kiln a shaft tapers to a hole at the top. At the foot of the kiln peat, wood and sometimes coal was used to ignite lumps of limestone, which were loaded into the kiln from the top, reached by a ramp. The resulting burnt lime was added to the soil to reduce its acidity, its calcium needed by the farm animals for healthy growth.

Selside, a tiny hamlet, was once the property of Furness Abbey and at one time it had an inn, a town hall and a fair. From here you can see a white track disappearing over a hill. This is the drove road over Cam Fell, walked by the Romans and traversed in walk 1. A small stretch of this ramble, around God's Bridge, was also traversed in Walk 1.

The commonest bird you will hear as you pass through Colt Park Wood nature reserve is the **willow warbler**. Its wonderfully sweet simple song seems to rise up and then, when full, run down the scale, expiring in a gentle murmur. It is a pleasing easily learnt song to start youngsters off on memorising bird calls and songs. In June hardly a minute passes that you will not hear the calls. Spotting the bird is more difficult. It is a little brown bird generally with, in spring, upper parts that are yellowish-olive. The feathers are margined with greenish-yellow. Its legs are brown.

The **chiffchaff** is another bird you will hear rather than spot. Its call is a repetition of two maybe three notes and from this it gets its name. It is another song that is easy to memorise.

WALKS WITH CHILDREN: RIBBLESDALE

4
Alum Pot and Long Churn, Selside

This is an exciting walk, with lots of interesting natural phenomena to see. Choose a sunny day if possible as the light on the limestone is a delight. A good time to go is during the summer half term when lots of youngsters from schools, the army cadets, or the scouts, descend the various potholes under the care of qualified instructors. They make a colourful sight in their bright thick suits and helmets as they queue to descend and then, suddenly, they are gone, underground, and the slopes are quiet and severe once more.

Start: A walled track, GR775756, that turns off, north, from the B6479, 2½ miles south from the B6255. Call at North Cote for permission to walk the private path to Alum Pot; a small charge is made for maintenance.

Total distance: 6.5km (4 miles)

Height gain: 90m (295ft)

Difficulty: Generally easy walk but take care on the clints and grikes and near to the potholes.

1. Walk up the walled track and, where it swings away to the left, take the stile beside the gate ahead. Beyond, follow a continuing track, which leads out onto the open moor, shadowed by Simon Fell, and then winds on towards an obvious clump of trees. Alum Pot lies below these and while enjoying this seemingly bottomless basin, youngsters should be reminded to take care. Cross the beck just beyond the pot and trend steadily right to the wall. Here is an unfenced entrance into part of Long Churn. Walk up beside the wall to a stiled fenced area to see more of Long Churn. There is a good view of an exit of the underground passageway and also of an entrance into the depths. Leave this fenced area by the far stile and walk up the slope onto a sea of limestone pavement, where again youngsters should be encouraged to tread carefully over the clints and grykes.

2. Bear left, soon to walk close beside a wall on your left. This brings you to a stile over a boundary wall. Beyond, bear right and carry on over some more splendid limestone pavement

WALKS WITH CHILDREN: RIBBLESDALE

and then a more grassy area to the edge of Upper Long Churn. Here you can see a passageway coming out of the fells and then a large basin-shaped hollow through which flows a stream. The water then descends as a waterfall, under a rowan, and disappears underground. A few metres beyond, is a very narrow entrance down to the passageway below and, sometimes, if there are potholers below, you can hear then talking. From here you may like to follow the line of the stream uphill for a short distance to come to Dr Bannister's 'washbasin' and Borrins Moor Cave from where potholers go under ground and walk through to Upper Long Churn.

3. Return the short distance to Upper Long Churn once again and then walk on along a narrow path, due south, to carry on parallel with the wall again, which lies to your left. Wind on round a stream bed and continue to a gate on your left, in the wall corner. This gives access to a grassy track. Walk downhill along the gated track for nearly half a mile to where the wall turns away left. Join a track and walk right for a short way and then leave the track, right, to a prominent ladder-stile over the wall. Continue across the next pasture to climb another ladder-stile. Wind round a fenced area and stroll on to pass through a gap in a wall ahead and on again through the next wall gap. Then follow a grassy track that leads to a gate, on the left. Pass beside South House farm and wind round, left, and then right, on the farm road to reach the B6479. Cross and go through the gate on the other side.

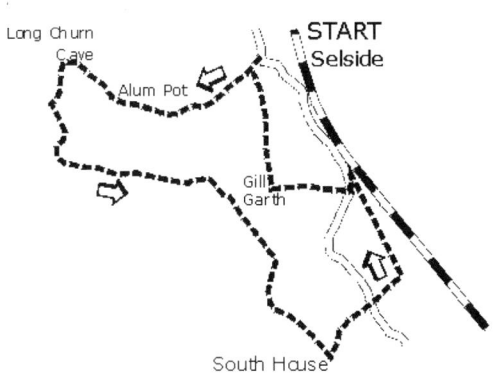

4. Walk ahead across the rough hilly pasture until the wall on the far side comes into view. Look here for an indistinct footpath and follow it left (northwards) to climb a stile. Go on through a wall gap and then descend a rough, slanting path down into a grassy valley. Climb up the other side

WALKS WITH CHILDREN: RIBBLESDALE

and bear diagonally left to the far corner to go through a gate and then a step stile to the roadside. Cross and walk back a short way to an obvious signposted footpath. Walk uphill to climb a stile over a fence. Then climb straight up to go through a gate in the wall corner. Carry on uphill to a ladder-stile on the top of the slope. Stroll ahead towards Gill Garth farm and before the dwelling bear right to climb a ladder-stile over the wall.

5. Pause here and look ahead over a grassy gill. Opposite is a fence and then, to its right, a wall. Near the first corner (right) in the wall is a good step stile that is difficult to spot. Descend the gill, climb the step stile and walk ahead to the next ladder-stile. Then bear steadily right to go through a wall gap and continue on to a very sturdy step stile in the corner, ahead. Beyond, bear left through a gate and then half right to a step stile over a fence and then right to a step stile to the walled track, where you have parked

Along the way

Alum Pot, near Selside, is a huge gash in the limestone fellside, nearly 100m deep. It is partly surrounded by a derelict wall. Pause here to look across the yawning gap to the beck beyond. At first the beck, when in spate, descends in white foam over a small drop in its bed and then it rages on to fall, with a roar into the depths. It flows on underground eventually passing below the River Ribble and then bubbling up into a small pool, Turn Dub. It then joins the Ribble from the opposite side to the pothole. This puzzling route was established by adding dye to the water. Leaning over the pothole are ash, rowan, Scots pine, sycamore and larch, all tall and bent by the wind.

Long Churn is a lengthy underground natural passageway stretching down the fell giving access to Alum Pot, about 30m from the top. The passageway can be accessed at several places along it.

Great care is needed on the **limestone pavement**. The slabs, (**clints**) are separated by crevices (**grikes**) sometimes several metres deep. In the crevices flourish a myriad of plants, including the long leaves of hart's tongue fern.

5
Horton in Ribblesdale, Sulber Nick and Crummack Dale

This is a walk for when adults think their youngsters are ready for a longer trek. Choose a spring day for this glorious stroll over the high limestone slopes and scars above Horton in Ribblesdale. This is the time when the ground nesting birds are in full song, when a myriad of tiny flowers spangle the grass and when you might see stoats and foxes on the move. Pick a sunny day, if possible, when the limestone appears even more bleached and pleasingly contrasts with the green of the sheep-nibbled turf.

Start: Horton village car park (GR808727)
Total distance: 13km (8 miles)
Height gain: 160m (520ft)
Difficulty: Good high-level paths. Those just above Horton can be muddy.

1. Go past the toilets, on the left, and cross the footbridge over the River Ribble. To your right is the fine old road bridge, still coping with huge lorries carrying slate from the quarries above. Beyond you can see The Crown Inn. Turn left to walk along the pavement. Go over Crag Hill Road and then climb the steep slope to Horton's railway station, which is bedecked in the colours of the Carlisle-Settle railway. Note the distances to Carlisle and London emblazoned on the platform. Cross the track, observing the warning notice. Climb steps to the left of a fence to a gate. Go ahead on the clear short path to go through another gate. Bear half right, with the quarry in view away to the left. Continue over the next stile into a large pasture and head on to climb a tall ladder-stile. Beyond, climb a short slope, right, and then continue on a pleasing terraced path. Pause here for magnificent views of a patchwork of pastures, edged with drystone walls, with Penyghent and its pronounced double scarp towering overall.

2. Follow the well-marked left turn (marked with blobs of red

WALKS WITH CHILDREN: RIBBLESDALE

paint and a boulder with a red arrow and FP) and begin to ascend through the limestone outcrops. The way is indistinct, but there are a few marker posts with yellow tops and some widely spaced cairns. Continue through limestone pavement,

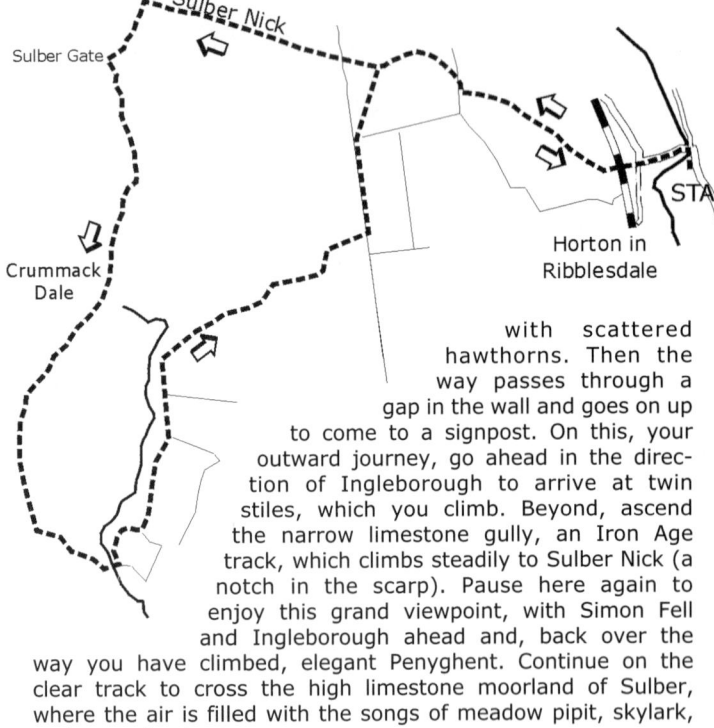

with scattered hawthorns. Then the way passes through a gap in the wall and goes on up to come to a signpost. On this, your outward journey, go ahead in the direction of Ingleborough to arrive at twin stiles, which you climb. Beyond, ascend the narrow limestone gully, an Iron Age track, which climbs steadily to Sulber Nick (a notch in the scarp). Pause here again to enjoy this grand viewpoint, with Simon Fell and Ingleborough ahead and, back over the way you have climbed, elegant Penyghent. Continue on the clear track to cross the high limestone moorland of Sulber, where the air is filled with the songs of meadow pipit, skylark, curlew and wheatear.

3. At the next signpost, set in a lonely hollow and with a vast limestone scar to your right, turn left. Walk the wide grassy way to Sulber Gate and take the ladder-stile to the right of the gate. Then, immediately, go through the small gate in the wall to your left. Pause once more to look down on a huge amphitheatre, enclosing a breathtaking sea of limestone. Move a few steps left and descend a narrow path to a grassy track below. Go ahead, with the evocatively named Thieves Moss to your left, tucked close up to a magnificent flaring

WALKS WITH CHILDREN: RIBBLESDALE

limestone scar. A short distance along, at a Y-junction of paths, take the less distinct one that bears off right and continues through this vast magical limestone area. Soon the path becomes distinct and there are several cairns. Eventually the way descends a small gully to come to Beggar's Stile, a tall ladder-stile through a high wall. Look for the ash tree just beyond, clinging precariously to the side of the scar.

4. Follow the grassy trod downhill to a finely cropped swathe coming in from right. Join this and go on towards a post. Here, just beyond a small pond, follow the yellow–topped marker posts leading you through Crummack Dale, with the pretty Austwick Beck – just emerged from a cave – meandering through the valley. The path brings you to a stile and gate in the boundary wall. Beyond, go ahead beside a continuing wall, with Crummack farm away over the pastures to your left. Waymarks take you through several sheep pens to join a bridleway. Stride this pleasant way for half a mile, before turning left along another good walled track in the direction of Wharfe.

5. This brings you to a picturesque clapper bridge over the Austwick beck – perhaps one of the oldest in the Yorkshire Dales. Here you will want to have your camera handy. Go on for a few yards, and then turn sharp left to begin your long walk through another superb walled track, flower–lined and generally grassy underfoot – unless the sheep have got in. This is Moughton Lane and is an old packhorse track from Austwick to Horton. The views ahead are superb. Remain on this track for well over a mile. As you go look across the vale to see Crummack farm again and then left to the waterfall where the Austwick Beck hurries out of its cave. This delightful track continues to a gate onto grassy slopes, just below Moughton Scars. Follow the track uphill to go through a gap in the limestone scar. Ignore a path going off left and another to the right and take an indistinct way, walking inland from the edge of the scar. Weave your way through the limestone outcrops to come to a faint Y-junction. Here keep to the right fork, with an old stone hut away to the left. Then look for several cairns and a row of butts, on either side of a clear track, stretching away, right, towards a long wall. The cairns and butts lead to a signpost and a ladder-stile, which you climb. Penyghent lies ahead.

6. Turn left and keep beside the wall, moving over shallow ridges of limestone before the way becomes grassy. Climb the

WALKS WITH CHILDREN: RIBBLESDALE

next ladder-stile and head on half right along a grassy trod towards a post. Beyond, you can see the signpost you passed on your outward journey. Turn right and continue downhill, bearing slightly right, along your outward route to return to Horton.

Along the way

The **quarry** is partially screened by trees and many more have been planted in protective sleeves. The limestone cliffs of the great hollows stand out dramatically in sunlight. There is noise from the quarry, but this serves to remind youngsters that the Yorkshire Dales are not just for walkers but have a working life too.

In 1876 the **Settle-Carlisle railway** reached Horton and quarrying developed. Today wagons and railway trucks carry the limestone all over the country. These are the wagons that walkers need to be aware of when using the B6479 in walk 2.

Limestones have been formed in ancient seas from the shell or skeleton remains of sea-creatures. These may be collections of shells cemented together, or maybe an accumulation of millions of tiny skeletons with some larger ones, or a mixture of these with calcium carbonate formed in the water.

Chalk is a soft limestone. Some organisms have a glass-like skeleton, which eventually provide material for flint, often found in chalk.

Look out for the **wheatear** perched on the drystone walls. Wheatear meaning white rump, does not feed on wheat! It is one of the first summer visitors to reach this country. It leaves again from August onwards, lingering for quite a time on the slopes and about the pastures. On the hills it nests holes in walls or clefts in rocks. Watch out for one that appears to disappear beneath a boulder, from where it will scuttle forward, in safety, to feed its young. In spring the male is pearl grey above, with a white forehead. Its underparts are a lovely sandy buff on the breast and flanks. It has some black parts too making it a most handsome bird.

WALKS WITH CHILDREN: RIBBLESDALE

6
Horton in Ribblesdale, Hull Pot and Hunt Pot

In sunshine the magnificent limestone walls around Horton in Ribblesdale glisten white where they criss-cross the fields and fells. Their solidity and permanence reflect the continuity of a peaceful, quiet way of life. This walk, which starts between these walls, takes you to see two magnificent potholes and their waterfalls.

Start: Horton in Ribblesdale village car park (GR808727)
Total distance: 9km (5½ miles)
Height gain: 120m (396ft)
Difficulty: Easy walking along the drove roads. *Take care as you approach the two potholes, where youngsters should be made aware of the dangers.*

1. Turn left out of the car park at Horton. Cross the road bridge and look left to see two more bridges over the wide and stately River Ribble. Turn right in front of the Crown Hotel and take the wide track off to the left, signposted 'Pennine Way' (PW). Stride out for 0.5km along the reinforced way – one of the many 'roads' used by drovers, packhorse trains, pedlars, travellers and shepherds.

2. Turn right through a metal gate and follow the wall on the right in the direction of the trees about Brants Gill Head. At the tumbledown wall that borders the ravine, walk left and go with it as it winds, right, round the great hollow. Cross the wall ahead, with the ravine below to your right. Pause here and look back to enjoy the view of the stream emerging from a dark cave before descending through the gill in three glorious cascades. Overhead, tower Scots pines, the dark foliage a perfect foil for several graceful larch and tall beech. Go on through the next two pastures to join another section of the PW.

3. Turn left to stroll the wide, walled way where it passes beside a small plantation of alder, larch and beech. The trees are soon left behind and the track takes you deeper into the lovely,

WALKS WITH CHILDREN: RIBBLESDALE

lonely, limestone countryside, with a spectacular view of Ingleborough to your left and Penyghent, much closer and to the right. Stroll on. Look over the wall on your right to see the dramatic Tarn Bar, a Malham Cove in miniature.

4. At the three-armed signpost, stride ahead on a wide grassy swathe – the PW swinging away right. Suddenly Hull Pot yawns ahead. Take care as the family approach and view – once the huge canyon was encircled by a protective wall but it now lies in small heaps of stones and there is no protection; a dramatic place to be avoided after dark and in dense mist.

5. Return along the grassy way to the three-armed signpost, turn left and continue on the PW. Just before the next wall a narrow path leads off right to the side of Hunt Pot, where a sparkling beck tumbles in many cascades over a series of ledges. It descends into a wide, grassy oval-shaped hollow, strewn about with large limestone boulders, before dropping over a ledge. Again all should take care here.

6. Return to the reinforced track and walk back to the three-armed signpost. Turn left to start the 2.5km walk back to Horton. Once past the gate, now on the right, from where you emerged from Brants Gill, continue on.

7. If you wish to visit the church, watch out for the track going off left. This leads you to a narrow lane where you turn right. Otherwise remain on the PW to join the B6479, where you turn right for the car park.

Along the way

This walk visits two **potholes**. These are holes gouged, or dug out, in the bed of a swift river or stream by sand or fine stones carried by the water. The river acts as a huge, whirling, scouring agent. The acid-laden water 'eats' its way through underlying weak spots between rocks cutting out caves, passages and waterfalls.

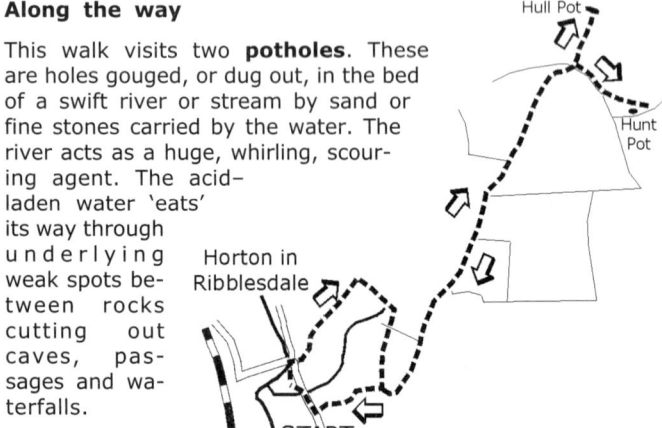

WALKS WITH CHILDREN: RIBBLESDALE

Meadow pipits, unconcerned by the chasm of **Hull Pot**, flit about the vegetation that hangs over the edge of the sheer sides of this collapsed cavern. After heavy rain Hull Pot Beck drops in a cloud of spray into the pothole, but when there is less water the beck disappears well before the lip. It emerges from a cave two–thirds of the way down the cliff face, where it falls in dancing white–topped cascades and then goes underground again.

The rugged ancient St Oswald's is known as '**the church on the Pennine way**'. It stands in the shadow of Penyghent. Look for the dog-tooth patterning on the stone arch over the south doorway and the magnificent Norman pillars and arches in the nave. Look too, for fragments of coloured glass in the western window, which might have come from a much larger picture in a window of Jervaulx Abbey. Notice the lychgates and the huge slabs of slate used for the path between them. These slabs will have come from the quarries close to Horton.

Many **packhorse routes** and drove roads were built in medieval times. These are now used by walkers on the PW and the Ribble Way.

On this walk you pass along tracks with **drystone walls** on either side. Almost all the walls would have been constructed two centuries ago by bands of itinerant wallers who wandered throughout the area seeking work. They earned about 12½p a day. Walls are more than just field boundaries, they provide shelter for sheep in bad weather and some were built to prevent sheep straying over precipices or into gullies where they might become crag-fast.

A sturdy wall has a good footing, usually square-shaped boulders set in two parallel rows, about 2 feet apart, in a shallow trench. The space between the two rows of footing stones was then filled with 'hearting' - small fragments of stone. More courses were then laid on this foundation, making sure that each stone rested on two stones in the course below, and again the space in between the two outside faces was filled with 'hearting'. Often 'through' stones were laid at intervals, these were stones which ran through the wall, projecting on either side, tying the two faces together. The more rows of throughs the stronger the wall. The top of the wall was completed with a row of 'cams' stacked on the top and all lying at the same angle. After building a wall the waller would often take a flying leap at it to test its strength. No mortar or cement was ever used.

7
Horton in Ribblesdale and foot of Penyghent

The pleasing path along the side of the River Ribble is in great contrast to Long Lane (track) which takes you up onto the moors above Helwith Bridge to the foot of Penyghent. If parents find the youngsters are getting tired on the long but gradual ascent, an energising drink or food might help, you could also remind them that from the foot of the Peak the way is all down – quite steeply down – seemingly for ever!

Start: Horton-in-Ribblesdale car park. (GR808727)

Total distance: 11.4km (7 miles)

Height gain: 290m (957ft)

Difficulty: This is a good walk for families to start aiming for the heights.

1. Leave the car park (north) by a metalled track behind cottages and to the right of the toilet block. Go over the footbridge across the River Ribble. Pause as you go to appreciate the well-proportioned road bridge which causes some grief to the wagons loaded with stone from the quarries. Just before the road, and at the end of the footbridge, take a gated stile, on the left, to descend to a meadow and join the Ribble Way. Carry on beside the lovely tree-lined river, which hurries by to your left. Cross a stile and walk a flagged path to go through a signposted gate. Descend steps and carry on. Away to your right, behind the Settle–Carlisle railway line and grassy slopes, you can see the first of the huge quarries, reminding you that this is not only a tourist paradise but also a working environment. Continue through the gated and stiled meadows. Enjoy the stretch where the path comes close to the river, here very wide and shallow. Then the path moves through a large stand of sycamores. Ignore the bridge across the Ribble and carry on. Go over a fine little cobbled bridge across a tiny tributary and head on through a gate to pass the outbuildings of Crag House farm. Ignore their bridge across the river too.

2. Beyond the gate continue on a wide track, beside the river,

WALKS WITH CHILDREN: RIBBLESDALE

where you might see dippers and grey wagtails. And then, just after a boundary wall across the pasture on your right, the river makes a large curve. Here head, right, across the large unsigned pasture to a ladder-stile over a wall. Climb a couple of steps right to continue on in the same general direction through a meadow, with a ditch to your left and the railway across the pasture to your right. Go across a gated tractor bridge over another ditch and walk ahead to go through a gap stile in the wall to come to the side of the lovely river once more. Turn right and walk on. Ignore the bridge on the left, and the stile on the right, and walk on along a walled track as it winds right to pass under a railway bridge. Go on through a gate onto a rough track and join a road. As this is used by slate and limestone wagons, walk left, circumspectly.

WALKS WITH CHILDREN: RIBBLESDALE

3. After 150m, take a signposted stile, in the wall, on the left. Climb a ladder-stile, cross the car park of the Helwith Bridge inn and then climb steps to the road. Bear left to cross Helwith Bridge over the Ribble and then go over the railway to come to the side of the B6479. Cross and turn left and walk on a couple of steps to join a walled rough track (Long Lane) climbing away from the busy road. You are still on the Ribble Way. Continue on the fine track as it climbs easily up onto the moors. At a junction of tracks, the Ribble Way turns away right. Ignore this turn and continue on the rising way, with fine views down into the Ribble valley and a marvellous view of the prow of Penyghent. After nearly two easy, gated miles from the junction you arrive at the Pennine Way (PW). To your right is the huge Churn Mill Hole, an enormous sink hole, which youngsters should view with care.

4. Turn left and walk the PW. Stride on a good track through heather, wavy hair grass, cotton grass and heath bedstraw. Continue on the duckboarded way to a step stile, almost under the famous peak. Continue on ahead, climbing steadily to a few metres before steps up the mountain. Here take either of the two ladder-stiles over the wall on the left. Beyond, join the wide path dropping down the slopes, keeping parallel with the wall to your right. This descends for 1¼ miles to the narrow road at Brackenbottom farm. There are several little scrambles down limestone outcrops that youngsters will enjoy; there is also an easy way around these outcrops for those of the family who opt for the less exciting way.

5. Turn right and walk the glorious shady lane to arrive at a charming group of houses. Pass the school and, just beyond a seat, cross a footbridge on the right. Turn right and walk a track as it swings left and climbs a small hill. At the next left turn, go through a small handgate beside a farm gate and descend another track to join the B-road. Cross and turn right to walk a few steps to the car park.

Along the way

Sink holes. Hard limestones are not porous but pervious, and rain water frequently passes through the many joints and enlarges them by solution. Beneath the surface, the water continues to pass down and along cracks and joints and these may in time create underground caverns, familiar to potholers. Along the courses of the surface drainage channels, the water may disappear through cracks which eventually be-

WALKS WITH CHILDREN: RIBBLESDALE

come larger and deeper and develop into sink holes. Collapse may leave gaping holes, partly filled with debris as seen at Churn Mill Hole.

The **Settle-Carlisle railway** accompanies you on the first part of the walk. Pause to watch the varying trains that hurry, dramatically, through the valley, carrying passengers or goods. In 1876 the railway line was brought to Horton and quarrying developed. Today limestone and slate are despatched, by road and rail, to many parts of the country.

Horton village is probably most famous for the starting point of the gruelling Three Peaks walk, which includes Ingleborough, Whernside and Penyghent, the latter is the lowest at 694m. Penyghent is sometimes described as looking like a crouching lion. Its characteristic stepped profile is due to the action of a glacier on its layers of carboniferous limestones, shales and sandstones. Horton's St Oswald's is known as the church on the Pennine Way. If you were unable to visit it at the end of walk 6, perhaps, after refreshments at the Penyghent Cafe you might fine time for a well worth visit at the end of this walk.

Penyghent Café. For over 30 years, walkers attempting the Three Peaks walk – three 700m mountains in a day – have been able to clock out and back at the café. If anyone hasn't made it back by the end of the day then the emergency services may be notified.

Delicate wavy hair-grass, seen on the walk as you approach Penyghent, has thin leaves and is very common. It flowers in June. Its Latin name is *Deschampsia flexuosa*, the latter word aptly describing the plant's stem.

Common cottongrass grows profusely over boggy ground or on wet moors. It is not really a grass but a sedge. It is a good indicator that the way ahead is wet and a detour is necessary. When you spot this lovely plant, with its long silky streamers being picked up by the breeze and carried away, it might be a good time to discuss plant indicators with youngsters.

Heath bedstraw grows on the hilly ground below Penyghent. It has tiny white stalked flowers, in small groups, that spring from a main stem. Up to six of these main stems arise from the root stock. Six tiny pointed leaves form a whorl around the stem and at intervals along it.

WALKS WITH CHILDREN: RIBBLESDALE

8
Stainforth and Catrigg Force

This is a great walk of contrasts. It starts from a charming village and then visits a magnificent waterfall. It goes on over high moorland pastures before returning beside deciduous woodland through which hurries another beck in fine cascades and waterfalls.

Start: Stainforth Pay-and-Display car park, (GR821673), where there are toilets. This lies on the edge of Stainforth just east of the B6479.

Distance: 7.4km (4½ miles)

Height gain: 120m (400ft)

Difficulty: Generally easy walking. *Care should be taken on the descent to see the waterfall.*

1. Turn right out of the parking area and follow the road as it swings right to cross the bridge over the Stainforth beck. Take the narrow gap immediately on the left, to walk beside the pretty beck. At the end of the path bear left to pass between dwellings to a small village green. Go on along the right side of the grass to the end of the tarmac to ascend the walled rough track, Goat Lane. It is steep at first but soon climbs steadily and pleasantly, giving ever-widening views of the fells.

2. Before the gate at the end of the track, take the stile on the left into a grassy area. Follow the narrow path down the slope to where it winds left, at a gate into beech woodland. Descend the sloping path with care, followed by stone steps (often slippery), to the bed of the ravine and the foot of the spectacular fall. Here, high up, the Stainforth descends over a lip into the immense hollow, in two majestic falls, one below the other, into a dark seething basin. All about the sides of the ravine grow fine trees and in high summer it is difficult to see to the top of the falls. Then the beck surges on to descend another drop in the riverbed. Here in this hollow youngsters should be under control as the current, after heavy rain, can be strong and the boulders about the foot of the ravine most slippery.

WALKS WITH CHILDREN: RIBBLESDALE

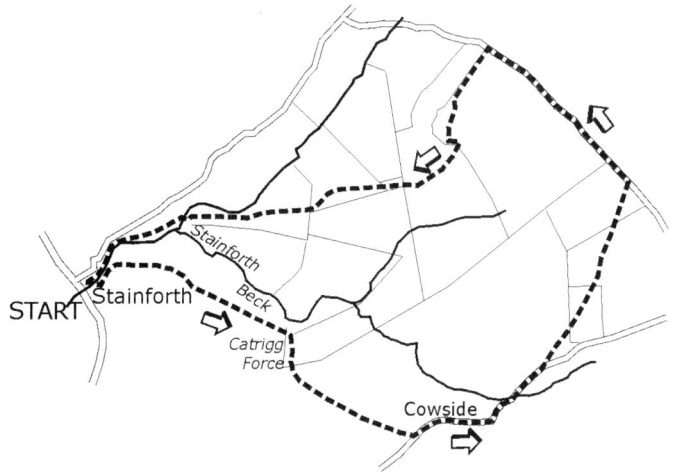

3. Return to Goat Lane, and climb the ladder-stile. Wind right and climb the slope to a gate and stile. From here there is a good view of Smearsett, Ingleborough, Penyghent and Fountains Fell. Beyond the stile, continue on the reinforced track to pass through a gate and walk on between limestone outcrops. Pass a limekiln on the right and dawdle on to a narrow moorland road.

4. Turn left, cross a cattle grid and descend below a row of lofty beech and horse chestnut. Pass the dwelling at Cowside and stroll on to go over a small bridge over Cowside Beck. Step out along the road to pass a copse of trees on the right and then, further on, another clump of trees on the left. Just beyond pass through a gate, on the left. Walk half right and go on in the same general direction over two stiles, then pass through a gate in the middle of a long fence. Carry on over a rather wet pasture to the next ladder-stile and then head on to take the right of two gates on to Henfield Road.

5. Turn left and walk the minor road until you reach a wall stretching away, on your left. Just before it, turn left onto a reinforced track. Follow this over Great Catrigg Pasture and go through the left of two gates. Carry on parallel with the wall to your right until your reach two ladder-stiles. Take the one to the right into a miry pasture. Walk on to climb the next ladder-

33

WALKS WITH CHILDREN: RIBBLESDALE

stile in the wall corner. Stride on along the hillock, then descend right and carry on beside the wall to a gate. Beyond, walk a track and, where it turns away right, go ahead to take a ladder-stile over a wall.

6. Descend right to the side of the fenced woodland about Tongue Gill Beck. If the trees are not in leaf you will have a fine view of the waterfalls before the beck descends into its very deep ravine and is lost to sight. Walk on down beside the woodland soon to join a good track that passes in front of a derelict barn to come to a concrete tractor bridge over the beck, which you cross. A few steps on Tongue Gill Beck adds its water to the Stainforth Beck in a most attractive confluence. Climb the track as it moves up a slope from where there is another good view of the confluence. Follow the track as it drops to a wide grassy area where the beck flows in a gracious curve. Go through a gate and stride on along the track and then turn left to walk downhill. Look left over a small green to see the fine stepping stones over the Stainforth Beck. Continue ahead where you might like to pass through the ornate gates to visit the lovely church. Then return through the gates, turn right and right again to the car park.

Along the way

Stainforth is divided in two parts by the River Ribble, the Settle–Carlisle Railway and the bypass. The church, St Peter's, is in Great Stainforth or Stainforth under Bargh as it used to be known (literally 'the stony ford under the hill'), and on the west bank of the river. Across the picturesque packhorse bridge, now owned by the National Trust, is Little or Knight Stainforth. If you have time to visit the church notice the colourful, tapestry kneelers. These were made by members of the congregation and friends, many as memorials to parishioners. Look also for the pleasing Millennium window, designed by Peter Kemplay and constructed by Hannah Glass of Leeds. 'Great' Stainforth is a quiet serene village. Once it was of much greater importance for it lay on the main packhorse route between Lancaster and York.

WALKS WITH CHILDREN: RIBBLESDALE

9
Stainforth Force, Langcliffe and Winskill

There is a remarkable variety of scenery on this walk. It takes in an elegant packhorse bridge, a magnificent waterfall, a long, beautiful stretch of tree–lined riverbank, two delightful villages, fine deciduous woodland, and pastures set high in limestone country.

Start: Stainforth Pay-and-Display car park, just off the B6479 (GR821674)

Total distance: 7.4km (4½ miles)

Height gain: 140m (460ft)

Difficulty: Easy walking on paths and tracks, with one steady climb and one steep descent.

1. From the car park entrance turn left, and then right, to walk (north) along the pavement of the B–road. When this runs out, cross with care, and continue on to a narrow left turn. Descend this pleasing way to cross the high-level railway bridge over the Settle-Carlisle railway and then drop down steeply to the go over the narrow packhorse bridge, over the River Ribble. At the far side of the bridge, on the left, climb through a gap stile in the wall to join the Ribble Way. Sturdy steps lead down to the roughish riverside path. From here look back towards the bridge, pleasingly reflected in the surging peat stained water. Walk on to come to the edge of Stainforth Force, where the Ribble cascades over limestone steps before racing over a shallow, wider ledge. It rages on to descend a much steeper fall in a flurry of foam, streaked with sienna, into a deep black pool. Beyond, the river widens and flows leisurely over its tree-shadowed rocky bed. Continue along the path to climb a ladder-stile into a wide, flat pasture.

2. Soon the path climbs high above the river and continues over a substantial step stile. Walk on along the glorious way and when you descend a row of steps after one of the several stiles along the riverbank, you come level with the Ribble once more. The path soon passes, on the opposite bank, a mill, one of several along this fine valley once making use of the river's

35

WALKS WITH CHILDREN: RIBBLESDALE

energy. To your right is a fine deciduous woodland. Carry on beside the woodland until you reach a splendid weir. Ignore the footpath, right, to Stackhouse, and turn left to cross the foaming water by the narrow bridge. Look for the fish pass, which allows trout and salmon to by-pass the turbulent water. Turn left, beyond the bridge, and walk the delightful narrow lane to the B6479, which you cross. Bear right and use the pedestrian bridge over the Settle-Carlisle railway line. Walk on for a 100m to the edge of Langcliffe village.

3. Bear left and walk between the very attractive houses and cottages to the large village green, with several seats just made for your first break. After a little exploration of the village, leave the green in the direction of the car park and, just before it, take a left turn along a reinforced track, Pike Lane. Follow this delightful walled way as it veers to the right and leads out of the village for nearly half a mile. Look ahead to see the superb limestone face of Stainforth Scar. Pass through a gate and carry on, right, along a raised grassy track. Ignore a gate on the right and go on under lofty ash. Beyond two gates, close together, follow the grassy trod to step through a gap in a derelict wall. Pause here and look back to enjoy the long views down Ribblesdale towards Settle. Carry on up under beech and then the path eases as it comes close to a walled deciduous woodland. Follow the path as it winds right to a small gate in the corner of two walls.

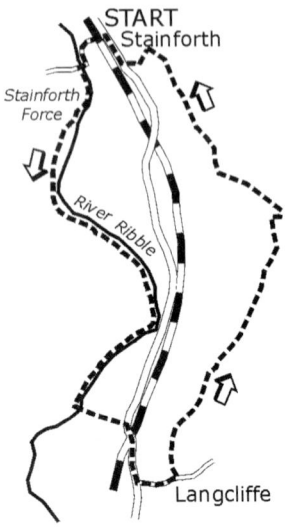

4. Beyond, climb the steepish slope, with scattered bushes about the way. Keep to the left of a large cairn, and go on, gently up, to walk ahead through a narrow walled pasture. Ignore a track to the left and, just beyond, climb a ladder-stile on your left. Once over, walk the clear path across a glorious buttercup meadow (in summer) to a gated stile onto a walled lane. Turn left and continue to Lower Winskill. Go between the dwelling and its outbuildings to pass through the gate

WALKS WITH CHILDREN: RIBBLESDALE

at the end of the yard. Head on towards a ladder-stile and then, beyond, bear right and, immediately, climb left up a short slope to join a wide grassy trod. Here walk right to climb the next ladder-stile, where there is a signpost. Pause again to enjoy the magnificent views. Carry on over the high-level pasture, in summer passing through a great variety of wild flowers. Stroll on towards the woods on Stainforth Scar and a stile.

5. Beyond, follow the stepped path (Cat Path) down through trees, to go through a gate out into a pasture. Continue on in the same direction through a sloping pasture. Go through the waymarked gate and then bear half left to a signpost and two boards, with 'footpath' written on them. Climb the ladder-stile to enter a small housing development, where you turn left to join the road. Walk right, then left and slightly right again if you wish to cross the stepping stones, or follow the road right and where it winds left to the car park.

Along the way

Langcliffe is a delightful, well kept village. Its church and 17th-, 18th-, and 19th-century cottages and houses surround its large green. It was rebuilt here, half a mile south-east of its original site, in a more defendable position, after marauding Scots, in 1315, razed the village to the ground. Langcliffe Hall, built in the 17th century as the ancestral home of the Dawson family was, in the early 20th century the home of Geoffrey Dawson, editor for seven years, of *The Times*. An earlier Dawson, Major William, was a friend of Isaac Newton (of the theory of gravity fame) who often stayed at the hall. The church, St John the Evangelist (1851), has a slender bell–turret and steeply pitched roof. Its tranquil and homely interior contains memorials to the distinguished Dawson family.

The **weir** was built to provide a head of water to drive a water mill. In the 18th century the mill became a corn mill, but by the 19th century it was converted to a cotton mill. It is now used for storage purposes.

Enjoy the summer flowers on the high limestone pastures, just north of **Lower Winskill**. Look, in late June, for rock rose, buttercups, pink clover, eyebright, lady's smock, wild mignonette, betony and pink orchids.

WALKS WITH CHILDREN: RIBBLESDALE

10
Attermire Scar and Victoria Cave

This is a charming walk and full of interest throughout. Pause often to enjoy the views and see how many hills the youngsters can name. In summer you will be walking through curlew and oyster catcher territory and you might even spot redshanks on the fell slopes. Summer is also the time to enjoy the wealth of flowers that thrive on the limestone soil. But at all times of the year this is a splendid walk though the wind can blow fiercely in front of the cave.

Start: Greenfoot car park, Settle (GR810634)
Total distance: 8km (5 miles)
Height gain: 190m (625ft)
Difficulty: Moderate. Several climbs but most on fine grassy paths.

1. Leave Greenfoot car park by the footpath that climbs steadily up the grassy slope, passes through a small copse and then continues by children's swings. Beyond the gate, turn right to walk a narrow stretch of road, with houses on either side. A few steps along swing steeply left, uphill, with the quiet green of Upper Settle to your right. Walk on through a very narrow way, lined with cottages. Follow it as the road moves out beyond the dwellings and continue beside a wall on your right, following a sign 'To the pinfold' and a 'No through road' sign. Ahead on the left is a pleasing stone walled enclosure, the pinfold, no longer holding stray animals but two bench seats and a picnic table, where, though a little early in the walk, you might like to pause for a break and enjoy the view over Settle.

2. To continue, turn left immediately before the pinfold and ascend the very steep short concrete track that leads beside a plantation, on the left, which almost encircles a small reservoir, where families should observe the warning signs. Beyond the stile over the track, walk on along a wide grassy swathe, which curves left and ascends easily to a step stile in the wall corner at the top of the pasture. Once over walk on a few steps to take a ladder-stile over the wall on your right.

WALKS WITH CHILDREN: RIBBLESDALE

Bear left following the wall on your left, which curves round the hill to your right. Remain parallel with the wall until you can climb a stone stepped stile. Then walk on still curving gently and remaining parallel with the wall to your left, to come to a signposted gate, which gives access to walled Lambert Lane (track), where you bear left and stroll the delightful way until you reach the Settle–Kirkby Malham road.

3. Turn right and, very soon, take the very narrow walled Stockdale Lane to your left. Where it turns sharply right, climb the ladder-stile on your left onto a wide, pleasant, grassy track that continues uphill beside the wall, on your right. Stroll the lovely way as it levels and carries on below Sugar Loaf Hill on your right. Follow the long grassy swathe downhill and also where it bears left, still descending, to a gate. As you drop down enjoy the dramatic limestone scenery all about you.

4. Beyond the gate, walk right along another fine grassy way and continue on to pass through a gateless gap. Then turn left to climb, with a wall to your left, ascending below magnificent Attermire Scar, where scree comes down almost to the edge of the now reinforced path. This leads you to a high plateau-like pasture, still with the scar flaring up to your right. Here some of the family might want to dance along the delightful way. Follow the clear path as it keeps to the right of a wall and brings you to a gate, with a board giving a warning about entering the cave ahead. Go through the gate and carry on now above the wall. From here you might spot Pendle Hill. A narrow path soon climbs right to the foot of Victoria Cave.

5. After viewing, with care, descend by a steeper path to the side of the wall once more and walk on to a gate, from where

you can see Ingleborough's flat crown. Beyond the gate, join a wide newly restored track, and turn left to go through another gate. Follow it downhill through pastures and then beside woodland. Cross the cattle grid and walk on to the end of the track at a corner of the fell road coming up from the village of Langcliffe. Bear left and in a couple of steps pass, left, through a gate in the wall, signposted Settle 1¼ miles.

6. Stroll ahead on the distinct path as it winds along beside the walled plantation and then across a pasture to pass through a gate to the right of a beech and sycamore copse. Look right, as you continue on the high-level, terrace-like way, to see Langcliffe village below. See if you can spot the River Ribble hurrying towards Settle. Carry on along the same contour. Then if in doubt over which gate of two you should take, go through the upper one and continue on to walk through a narrow walled pasture to go through a gate. Pass through the next meadow and then the path funnels you into a descending walled track, Banks Lane. At the time of writing, this was very rough, but work was just starting to improve the surface.

7. At the end of the lane, join a metalled road. Follow this left and then right to descend to Settle, where you may like to enjoy its many interesting shops. Turn left for the car park and go on ahead, squeezing through the narrow roads if it is market day.

Along the way

Pinfolds were pounds for stray cattle. They were stone walled enclosures, open to the sky, where the cattle or sheep would remain until they were claimed by their rightful owners. The word pound comes from *impound* which means to shut up in an enclosed space.

Once **Victoria cave**, a huge cavern, could be entered only by a slit. Later its entrance was enormously enlarged during various exploratory archaeological digs. All the family should heed the warnings not approach too close or enter the cave because of the danger of falling rocks and deep shafts.

There seems to be some doubt who first discovered the cave. One source suggests it was found by **a Michael Horner**, in 1838, while walking on the public holiday given for the coronation of Queen Victoria. The legend on the information board by the cave suggests that a dog, in 1837, sent in after a fox lead to its discovery.